CIA & FBI

FIGHTING TERRORISM

David Baker

Rourke
Publishing LLC
Vero Beach, Florida 32964

www.rourkepublishing.com

PHOTO CREDITS: p. 36: Bettmann/Corbis; p. 43: Dennis Brack-Pool/Getty Images; p. 31: David Burnett/Getty Images; pp. 7, 16, 18, 33: Corbis; p. 30: Bob Daemmerich/AFP/Getty Images; p. 26 (Tech. Sgt. Cedric H. Rudishill): Department of Defense; p. 4: Chris Fairclough/Chris Fairclough Worldwide Ltd; pp. 8, 9 (t), 13, 20, 21, 22, 23, 25, 28, 29: Federal Bureau of Investigation; p. 38: Getty Images; p. 11: Hulton Archive/Getty Images; p. 34: Imperial War Museum; p. 19: Keystone/Getty Images; pp. 9 (b), 12: Library of Congress; p. 10: MPI/Getty Images; p. 15: Alessia Paradisi/AFP/Getty Images; p. 40: Paul J. Richards/AFP/Getty Images; p. 41: Brendan Smialowski/Getty Images; p. 14: Three Lions/Getty Images; p. 37 (Staff Sgt. Matthew Hunner): U.S. Air Force; p. 39 (Sgt. Kevin R. Reed): U.S. Marines; p. 24 (Petty Officer 3rd Class Isaac D. Merriman): U.S. Navy; p. 5: Mark Wilson/Getty Images

Title page picture shows an FBI SWAT team in training.

Produced for Rourke Publishing by Discovery Books
Editor: Paul Humphrey
Designer: Ian Winton
Photo researcher: Rachel Tisdale

Library of Congress Cataloging-in-Publication Data

Baker, David, 1944-
  CIA and FBI / by David Baker.
     p. cm. -- (Fighting terrorism)
  Includes index.
  ISBN 1-59515-482-5
  1. United States. Central Intelligence Agency--Juvenile literature. 2. United States. Federal Bureau of Investigation--Juvenile literature. 3. Intelligence service--United States--Juvenile literature. 4. Terrorism--United States--Prevention--Juvenile literature. 5. September 11 Terrorist Attacks, 2001--Juvenile literature. I. Title: Central Intelligence Agency and Federal Bureau of Investigations. II. Title. III. Series.
  JK468.I6B35 2006
  363.320973--dc22

                    2005028011

Printed in the USA

TABLE OF CONTENTS

Chapter One

Making the Nation Safe

Today, we all take for granted the good feeling that comes from living in a country where law-abiding citizens go about their daily lives in relative safety. We all want to be able to live without

Police officers on patrol in New York City. In America, we rely on all our law enforcement agencies to protect us from terrorist attacks.

fear of attack or violence. This brings a feeling of security because we know that state and federal law enforcement officers are ready to pounce on those who try to harm us. Of course, there can never be total security because we will never completely eliminate those who believe they can take by force the things the rest of us have to work for.

There are some who want to destroy our way of life, if only through jealousy or envy. Some of those people work from inside our own country while others work from faraway places to undermine the freedoms of the United States. Today we can be secure in the knowledge that there are two organizations that work inside and outside the 50 states to insure the freedoms we have worked and fought to secure for more than 200 years. These organizations are the Federal Bureau of Investigation, or FBI, and the Central Intelligence Agency, the CIA. They have not always been there.

The seal of the Federal Bureau of Investigation.

Chapter Two

The Federal Bureau of Investigation

The history of our security services tells us a lot about our country. Never wanting to build big government organizations when things could be settled at local level, nevertheless there came the day when America was growing too fast for all the policing to be handled at the state level. By the beginning of the 20th century the country was a rapidly expanding industrial nation. It was exporting manufactured goods and products all over the world. It was simply getting too big for local policing as the only means of law enforcement.

By the turn of the 20th century America was growing very rapidly and some sort of federal law enforcement agency was needed. This picture shows the Lower East Side of New York City around 1900.

Sometimes criminals would dash across state or national borders, performing criminal acts in one place and escaping to another. Something was needed to allow law officers to move across boundaries and seek out the criminals and gangsters wherever they fled. An organization was needed that would

reach out beyond state or national boundaries to pursue the criminal. This organization would eventually become the FBI. But it did not begin as that. Problems with maintaining law and order across boundaries were discussed by President Theodore Roosevelt and Attorney General Charles Bonaparte in 1908, when moves began to set up the organization that would become the FBI. Roosevelt and Bonaparte were both **Progressives** who believed that efficiency and expertise, not

The first Department of Justice building, in Washington, D.C., which served as the headquarters of the attorney general and his staff from 1899 to 1917. The Bureau of Investigation, the forerunner of the FBI, was also housed in this building.

political connections, should determine who should serve in government.

By 1907 the Department of Justice was using Secret Service operatives to carry out investigations across state borders. Formed in 1865 by Act of Congress as an agency of the Department of Treasury,

President Theodore Roosevelt (left) and Attorney General Charles Bonaparte (above) discussed the setting up of a federal law enforcement agency early in the 20th century.

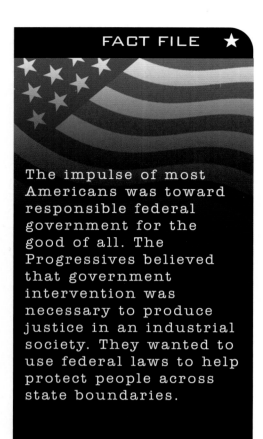

The impulse of most Americans was toward responsible federal government for the good of all. The Progressives believed that government intervention was necessary to produce justice in an industrial society. They wanted to use federal laws to help protect people across state boundaries.

the Secret Service had been set up to fight **counterfeiting** of U.S. currency. After the **assassination** of President McKinley in 1901, it was given the additional job of protecting the president. Secret Service men were fit, well trained, and reported to the Chief of the Secret Service.

The anarchist Leon Czolgosz assassinated President McKinley in 1901. Following this incident, the Secret Service took on the role of protecting the president.

Chapter Three

The Lawless Years

Within a few years of its formation in 1908, the Bureau of Investigation (BOI) had a staff of 600, half of them Special Agents. When President Woodrow Wilson took America to war in 1917 the Bureau acquired responsibility for **espionage**, acts

Federal agents dispose of illegal liquor during Prohibition. The illegal sale of liquor became one of the principal activities of organized crime during the 1920s and early 1930s.

of **sabotage**, and for helping the Department of Labor get rid of enemy aliens. With peace in 1918 came resumption of normal duties.

During the so-called lawless years of 1921-1933, the Bureau fought **gangsterism**. It also opposed the public disregard for **Prohibition**, which made it illegal to sell or import intoxicating beverages. On May 10, 1924, Attorney General Harlan Fiske Stone appointed J. Edgar Hoover to head the Bureau of Investigation.

In 1929 the stock market crash brought a money crisis to the United States known as the Great Depression. In hard times crime thrives and creates more criminals. To combat this wave of crime the new president, Franklin D. Roosevelt (elected in 1932), fought hard to put an end to lawlessness. He encouraged

Attorney General Harlan Fiske Stone, the 52nd Attorney General, served from April 1924 to March 1925. He later became Chief Justice of the Supreme Court.

J. Edgar Hoover headed the FBI from 1924 until his death in 1972.

the BOI to take its anti-crime message to the people and approved greater resources for it to expand its activities.

In 1935 the BOI was renamed the Federal Bureau of Investigation, and the modern FBI was born. By 1936 new powers under law gave the FBI the chance to clean up the streets and end gangsterism. By this time, however, a new set of threats had emerged outside the United States.

A march of American fascists through the streets of New York City during the 1930s. The FBI was charged with the task of investigating fascist and communist groups during the years before World War II.

In Italy fascism had turned the country into a dictatorship under Mussolini. In Germany Nazis under Hitler were threatening to wage war. In Russia, Stalin's communists openly preached world domination. Any one of these threats could interfere with the freedoms of the American people and bring war once more to the world.

The FBI began to turn its attention to threats from outside the country that could endanger Americans at home. President Roosevelt authorized Secretary of State Cordell Hull to investigate fascist and communist organizations in the United States. During the mid 1930s the economy was still depressed. This bred violent groups that wanted to overthrow the government and make arrangements with fascists in Europe or communists in Russia.

The FBI played a large part in seeking out these groups and stopping their violent activity. By the end of the 1930s the FBI had grown to a total force of almost 1,800 people, of whom 654 were special agents operating out of 42 cities.

Chapter Four

New Threats

The modern terrorist is nothing new. He or she comes in many different forms. There is the suicide bomber who blows up targets and dies in the explosion. There is the cowardly criminal who sends letter bombs to important people—or just anyone at random. Then there is the terrorist who works quietly for years waiting for the opportunity to cause death and destruction. These people can be living inside the United States or in a foreign country.

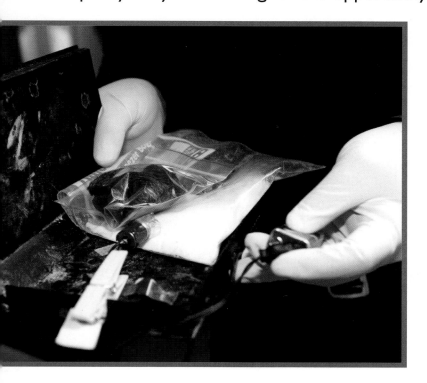

Letter bombs, like this one hidden in a videocassette case, are just one of the many deadly weapons available to the modern terrorist.

The Japanese attack on Pearl Harbor in December 1941 brought America into World War II and led to an expansion of the role of the FBI.

Fear of people attempting to destroy or attack the country from within really began many decades ago. When America was attacked without warning by Japanese naval forces striking at Pearl Harbor, Hawaii, in December 1941, there were many Japanese people living in the United States. Some were suspected of plotting terrorist activities, and these people were arrested by the FBI and turned over to the authorities.

Now the FBI had another activity by protecting the American people from internal terrorism, known as **subversive** activity. They still carried out their civil role against criminals, but the new, less obvious, threat needed more people. By 1943 the FBI had more than 13,000 employees including 4,000 agents. Most of these worked in what had now become the traditional role of the FBI. Some, however, were separated out and worked in a new organization known as the Special Intelligence Service, or SIS. Set up in 1940 by President Roosevelt, its job was to seek out people and companies in Latin and South America working for the Nazis.

When the war ended in 1945, there were new threats of a different kind. It was now a world in which the atom bomb threatened world peace. The FBI needed new tools for these new threats to freedom and democracy. Scientific methods became available after the war, when communist Russia, the Soviet Union, posed a threat to the United States, during a period known as the **Cold War**.

The Soviet leader Stalin had said in 1946 that wars were going to keep happening until communists ruled the world. The Soviet Union did its best to

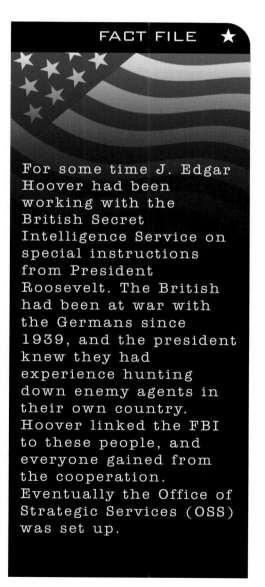

FACT FILE ★

For some time J. Edgar Hoover had been working with the British Secret Intelligence Service on special instructions from President Roosevelt. The British had been at war with the Germans since 1939, and the president knew they had experience hunting down enemy agents in their own country. Hoover linked the FBI to these people, and everyone gained from the cooperation. Eventually the Office of Strategic Services (OSS) was set up.

The dropping of an atomic bomb on the Japanese city of Nagasaki on August 8, 1945 helped bring about the end of World War II, but it also ushered in an era of fear and suspicion known as the Cold War.

destroy freedom and liberty in many places in eastern Europe, in Africa, in the Middle East, and in Southeast Asia. Stalin died in 1953, but his successors survived until the end of the 1980s. Then the Russian people marched against communism, and the old communist leaders were brought down.

During the period when communists were in power, the Soviet Union supported groups that wanted a communist style leadership in America. The FBI used several different methods to identify the people who were in these groups and to watch them. Although few Americans wanted to overthrow the government, the threat was real and taken seriously by the FBI. Gradually, over the decades of the 1960s and 1970s, these people were identified, and some were sent to jail for long periods.

Because America is an open society, it was relatively easy to gain information, knowledge that was vital to terrorists and to

During the Cold War the Soviet Union held eastern Europe in a vise-like grip. When the government of Czechoslovakia attempted to bring that country toward democracy in 1968, Soviet tanks soon moved into Prague, the capital city.

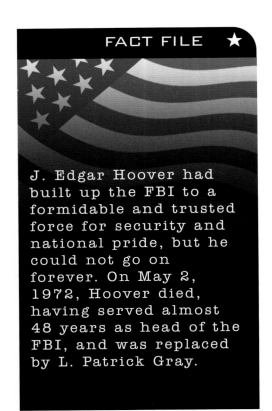
the agents of foreign powers or fanatical gangs. The FBI worked tirelessly to root out these people. The fact that the FBI is an independent agency answerable only to the president through the Justice Department helped it work free from interference. It could go where it wanted and never assume that any organization was entirely innocent.

The J. Edgar Hoover Building, the present-day headquarters of the FBI, on Pennsylvania Avenue, Washington, D.C.

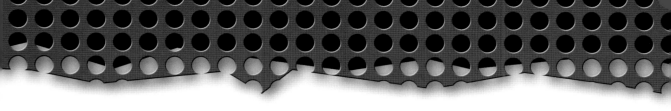

Chapter Five

The Bombers

By the early 1990s the Soviet Union had collapsed, and the new Russia said it would hold free elections on the road to democracy. The world was no longer under the immediate threat of nuclear war. Russia and America made pledges to work together to make the world a safer place. Some people believed it

The 1990s brought the end of the Cold War and the beginning of terrorist attacks on American soil. This is the aftermath of the 1993 attack on the World Trade Center in New York City. The explosions killed six and wounded hundreds.

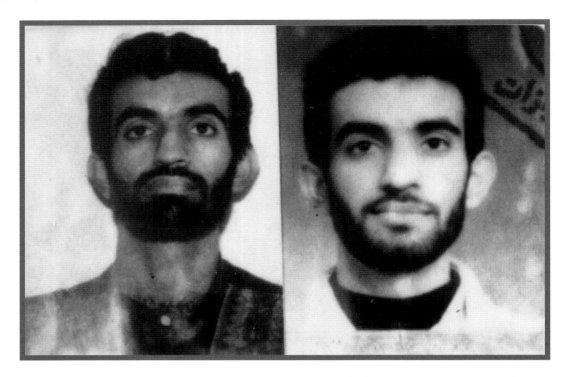

FBI pictures of terrorist bomber Ramzi Yousef. Following his arrest, trial, and conviction on terrorist charges he is now held at the high-security Supermax prison in Florence, Colorado.

would be a new age of peace and prosperity, but some believed the world was in greater danger. They said that fanatical groups held back by strong rulers toppled from power would make war against America and her allies.

Sadly, it seemed they were right. No sooner had the Russian threat gone away than others stepped up to challenge the free world. In a series of bombings that shook America into renewed action, the FBI was faced with yet another type of enemy. These enemies would work from both inside and outside the United States to kill hundreds or perhaps thousands of people at the same time.

In 1993 a man using the name Ramzi Yousef put together a bomb designed to topple the World Trade Center in New York City. Yousef had entered the United States on an Iraqi passport. Had he succeeded, several thousand people would have died. As it turned out, six died but the bomb did not bring down the building.

Two years later Yousef and his henchmen were at it again. In 1995 they attempted to build a bomb to blow up eleven airliners in one spectacular day of rage. As Yousef was assembling the device made of liquid explosive, he accidentally started a fire. Running in panic, he fled from the building. He left behind incriminating information on a computer. One month later he was arrested in Pakistan and brought to trial in the United States. Evidence was gathered from the intelligence agencies and the FBI.

In the same year that Yousef was arrested, an extremist in America, Timothy McVeigh, drove a rental truck packed with explosives to the Murrah Federal Building in downtown Oklahoma City. When it blew up, it tore off half the nine-story building. For nearly two weeks rescue workers pulled people from the rubble. The bomb had killed 168 men, women, and children.

Terrorism does not always come from abroad. On April 19, 1995, Timothy McVeigh and Terry Nichols left a truck bomb outside the Murrah Federal Building in Oklahoma City. Nichols was convicted of manslaughter and sentenced to life imprisonment. McVeigh was sentenced to death and executed in 2001.

Events like this told the intelligence services that the threat from terrorism was real. To combat these threats, the FBI uses the latest technology. At about this time the **electronic** age had made it possible to tap into people's telephone conversations using **remote** listening and to record conversations. With the detailed records the FBI had gathered together, it became possible to link people with their actions. When checked against

An FBI agent checks the voice recorder from crashed Egypt Air Flight 990 in November 1999. An investigation by the National Safety Transportation Board concluded that the co-pilot had deliberately crashed the plane.

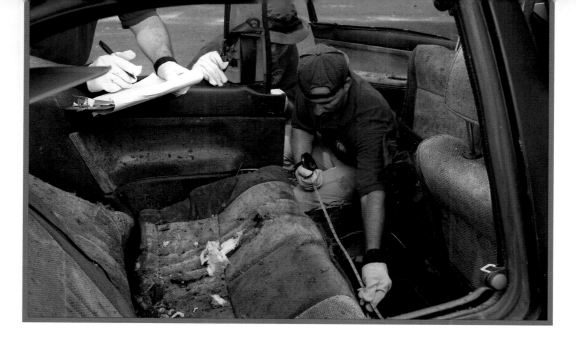

Agents at the FBI's Academy in Quantico, Virginia, take measurements in a car after a simulated bomb blast. These measurements can be used to reconstruct the bomb and the incident and help to determine the type of bomb used.

fingerprint records, it was possible to link places (where the fingerprint was found) to people. In this way technology is able to improve security by tracking terrorists before they strike.

The FBI also uses advanced communications systems. With **satellites** and high-powered Internet links, the FBI can send this information wherever it is needed, in this country or abroad. The FBI has become a national law enforcement intelligence service that is vital in the fight against terror. It can send information to police officers anywhere in the country. If it finds a link between terrorist activity and individuals in its records, the local police can be involved in the case.

The FBI can also link up with police forces in other countries that want to help in the war on terrorism. To help build a world in which all law enforcement agencies are able to cooperate, the FBI has set up schools in other countries. These International Law Enforcement Academies are located in Hungary and Thailand and teach several hundred police officers each year.

Chapter Six

The Events of 9/11

On September 11, 2001, terrorists who had infiltrated the United States performed the most horrific act of terror ever on American soil. On that day two hijacked airliners rammed into each of the World Trade Center twin towers in New York City. A third aircraft was hijacked and flown into the Pentagon

building near Washington, D.C. A fourth airliner that may have been aimed at the White House was brought down in countryside far short of its intended target by passengers who overwhelmed the hijackers. It crashed in an empty field in Shanksville, Pennsylvania, killing all on board.

Infamously, this day is remembered by its abbreviated date as 9/11. On that fateful day almost 3,000 people died at the three sites. These events changed the FBI more than any event since it had been formed in 1908. After 9/11 the prevention of further terrorism became the agency's top priority. Its second priority was to protect the United States against foreign intelligence operations (known as **counterintelligence**) and against espionage. For decades America had been subjected to attack at its embassies and military bases abroad, but this was the most devastating attack against the continental United States in its history.

The FBI set up protection against electronic crimes, also known as cyber-based attack. Before 9/11 the FBI had concentrated on cyber-crime carried out by criminals in the

> **FACT FILE** ★
>
> Counterintelligence is when someone or some country tries illegally to obtain classified information. It also includes sabotage, assassinations, and acts of terrorism. Counterintelligence was used widely by communist Soviet Russia during the Cold War, and its practices have been adopted by terrorists.

(Opposite) FBI agents, firefighters, rescue workers, and engineers work at the Pentagon crash site on September 14, 2001, where a hijacked American Airlines flight had slammed into the building on September 11.

An FBI SWAT team in training. Such teams will be used to round up suspected terrorists operating on American soil.

United States. With the new wave of terrorism, it also set up programs and offices to stop terrorists using these methods to attack the United States. Terrorists could use illegal electronic methods to obtain cash illegally from banks and financial institutions. The FBI set up a Terrorism Financing Operations Section to combat this activity.

In addition to stopping the illegal transfer of funds, the FBI could also turn its sights on the terror organizations by cutting off their own supply of funds. Money buys explosives, bombs, and equipment to wage terror. By hunting down their means of getting money, the FBI was able to starve these organizations of resources.

The month after 9/11, President George W. Bush issued instructions for the FBI to create a Foreign Terrorist Tracking Force. This hunts down people living illegally in the United States and tracks people trying to get into the country who are known to sympathize with terrorists.

In 2002 a new law was passed that allowed checks on people who want to use dangerous biological agents and harmful products, or **toxins**. Toxins can maim or kill and are one of the weapons used by terrorists to create fear. Among these is **anthrax**, which can spread quickly and cause panic.

Attention to all these activities grew fast after the first attacks on the World Trade Center in 1993 and the attack on the Murrah Federal Building in 1995. In 1996 the Bureau committed 10 percent of its workforce to counterterrorism. In 2003 that commitment had grown to 43 percent of the total workforce.

FBI agents wearing "moon suits" during a chemical weapons exercise in Portland, Oregon.

Chapter Seven

The Central Intelligence Agency

In the fight against terrorism there are two essential weapons. The first is an effective federal intelligence agency capable of controlling people who come in to the country, if they are plotting murderous acts of terror, and where they can be found. This organization must have powers of arrest. That is the FBI. Second, there has to be an efficient international intelligence service capable of reaching around the globe and seeking out those who plan acts of murder and mass terror. This is the Central Intelligence Agency, the CIA. Today it is one of the most

The seal of the Central Intelligence Agency.

The outside of the present CIA headquarters in Langley, Virginia.

important agencies in the fight against U.S. enemies in general and against terrorists in particular. Operating throughout the world, the CIA is a general source of global information, with much of its information base available to the general public. The CIA is also responsible for monitoring activities likely to threaten the security interests of the United States and her allies. The CIA also controls the flow of information about countries capable of threatening the United States with conventional, nuclear, or biological weapons.

The CIA is not as old as the FBI; it was put together after World War II out of experiences with intelligence gathering during the war against Nazi Germany in Europe and against Japan in the Pacific.

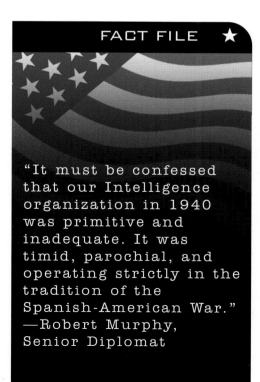

FACT FILE ★

"It must be confessed that our Intelligence organization in 1940 was primitive and inadequate. It was timid, parochial, and operating strictly in the tradition of the Spanish-American War."
—Robert Murphy, Senior Diplomat

Chapter Eight

First Steps to a New Service

Before World War II, the U.S. government got its intelligence information from the Department of State and the armed services. The Office of Naval Intelligence (ONI) and the War Department's Military Intelligence Division (G-2) fed details from their contacts all around the world to higher authorities, sometimes even to the desk of the president. But no one below the White House level of decision making put together, or collated, all the different strands of information.

In the late 1930s, as war loomed in Europe, President Roosevelt did what he had asked the FBI to do: to work with British intelligence officials to set up a new organization that would provide an over-all assessment of intelligence information. The president wanted nothing short of a special group to make meaningful sense of all the different pieces of information. In July 1941, Roosevelt appointed William J. Donovan as Coordinator of Information (COI).

The Japanese attack on Pearl Harbor on December 7, 1941, caused a major rethink about the gathering of intelligence information. This dramatic day in America's history caused

increased work for the FBI, but the COI was affected even more. After all, was it not a lack of intelligence that had allowed the Japanese naval forces to attack without warning?

On June 13, 1942, the Office of Strategic Services (OSS) was set up, with Donovan at its head. Donovan formed five separate divisions within the OSS. SI gathered secret intelligence from foreign governments. SO carried out operations such as sabotage and concealed attacks on the enemy. There was a Research and Analysis division, which carried out analyses of upcoming military operations.

And there was a Morale Operations division that broadcast propaganda into Nazi-occupied Europe. A group known only as X2 operated as spy hunters, tracking down German "stay-back" units left behind as the Allies advanced across Europe and the Nazis retreated.

Learning from the British, who had been at war since 1939 and were applying sabotage tactics of their own, the OSS was a highly effective fighting force for concealed warfare. This secret,

or concealed, warfare gave the OSS much experience in sabotage and information gathering that would later be helpful to the CIA in protecting the United States during the Cold War and the new threats from terrorism. In particular, X2 had access to the decoded signals from enemy radio communications that allowed them to plan espionage and conduct subversive activities.

The OSS was modeled after the British Special Operations Executive (SOE). This photo shows an SOE wireless operator at work, probably in German-occupied France.

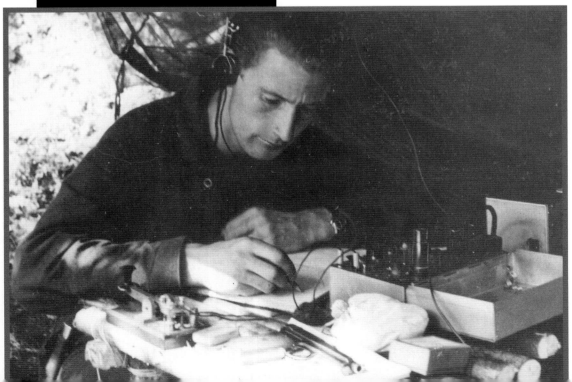

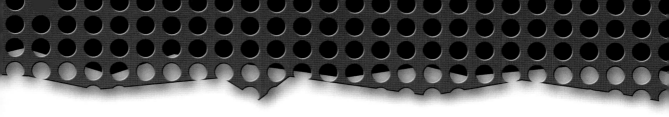

Chapter Nine

The Cold War and After

On May 8, 1945, the war in Europe ended, and on September 2 Japan surrendered **unconditionally**. With the coming of peace there was no further need of the OSS. It was disbanded on October 1, but the SI and X2 branches were saved to form the nucleus of a new peacetime intelligence service. That service came into force with the National Security Act that became law on December 18, 1947, the date the Central Intelligence Agency opened for business.

At first the work involved attempts to find out the intentions of the Soviet Union. Its leader, Stalin, had failed to live up to his promise that people in eastern Europe liberated from Nazi occupation would be given a free vote for the government of their choice.

Within two years the Soviet Union stopped access to Berlin in East Germany, and in 1950 communist forces in North Korea attacked South Korea. The United Nations agreed to send a force to push back the communists to North Korea, and for three years the war raged until that was achieved. Around the world it seemed the communists were attempting to smash their way to domination of democratic countries.

Following World War II, Berlin was divided into a communist east and a democratic west. In August 1961, this division became concrete, when the communists built a massive wall across the city.

A priority for the national security of the United States and for the assistance sought by free nations was to gather high quality intelligence about Soviet and Chinese communist intentions. There was also a need to use any technical means possible to find out about Soviet and communist Chinese military power.

By the early 1950s the CIA had grown to be a major source of information about the strength and capabilities of many countries in the world. Throughout the Cold War, the CIA used a wide range of technical means to gather intelligence.

Special aircraft were designed, like the U-2 spy plane that began flying secret missions over the Soviet Union on July 4, 1955.

By 1962, when the Soviet Union secretly placed nuclear missiles on Cuba, the U-2 had mapped almost all the Soviet Union. The U-2 was the first to tell intelligence officials about the surprise missile deployment on America's doorstep. Within hours President John F. Kennedy had the information on his desk.

What unfolded over the next days and weeks became known as the Cuban Missile Crisis. It took the world to the brink of war, but intelligence information gave the U.S. leadership the right details to take action that would force the Soviets to withdraw and prevent war. Without those details the situation would have been made worse by uncertainty and could have resulted in the world's first nuclear conflict.

Even when the Cold War ended in 1989, the CIA still had an important job to do. All the skills acquired during the 45 years of

The U-2 spy plane is still in action today, over fifty years after its first spying missions. The U-2 helped the CIA discover what was going on in countries considered hostile to the United States.

This photo taken from the air shows the ballistic missile base on Cuba, which sparked the Cuban Missile Crisis of October 1963.

tension with Soviet communism were applied to new challenges. Terrorism began to increase around the world, and the CIA extended its reach into remote regions.

Seeking those who committed violence against Americans, and working with its allies, the CIA developed technical resources to gather information about these people. Spy satellites and aircraft equipped with special **surveillance** gear were used around the world where threats emerged.

The CIA did what it does best and gathered highly detailed information, tracked suspicious individuals, and collected evidence on terror organizations and bands of criminals determined to undermine free and democratic processes.

This data enabled the U.S. political leadership to make important decisions and helped decide action to constrain or eliminate the threat. Sometimes this means going to war in order to prevent even greater death and destruction. Intelligence is a vital part of knowing the facts before deciding what to do.

It was intelligence information about the possible presence of weapons of mass destruction in Iraq that triggered the U.S.-led invasion of that country in 2003.

Chapter Ten

Collective Intelligence

There are 15 separate sources from which the U.S. government gets intelligence information. The most important of these is the CIA, but the others have vital roles to play. Some are involved in deciding whether to use military action and to provide armed forces with important information that helps cut casualties. Others provide information about nuclear, chemical, or biological devices that can be turned into weapons.

The CIA's Director of Intelligence Porter J. Goss (right) confers with FBI Director Robert Mueller at the National Counterterrorism Center in Tysons Corner, Virginia, June 2005.

The 9/11 Commission Report found serious gaps in the CIA's intelligence gathering network before the terrorist attacks of September 11, 2001.

All this information is essential for a properly managed government responsible to the people for their safety and well-being. In November 2004 a new post of Director of Intelligence was created to combine all these different sources. In this way the information and data assembled by all these organizations can be used most effectively and efficiently. In turn, that will ensure that anti-terrorist departments of the FBI and CIA are now better equipped than they have ever been to protect vulnerable citizens and the principles of free and democratic government.

In the wake of the terrifying attacks of September 11, 2001, a special commission was appointed to examine the performance of the intelligence communities in the United States. On behalf of the American people they represented, Congress wanted to know whether there could have been any warning and if the intelligence services could have done anything to prevent these events.

In a joint assessment published openly by the House of Representatives and the Senate, the Commission found serious gaps in the intelligence information and in the way intelligence gathering had been handled. It did not state that any one person had directly avoided responsibility, but it did claim that some sections of the CIA and other intelligence services were badly managed and poorly led.

The report also found that the problems had not been the sole responsibility of the administration in power when the attacks happened. It concluded that for several decades successive governments had failed to keep pace with the developing threat from terrorism and that the intelligence services had not been properly reorganized for new threats after the Cold War.

It also said that the way the intelligence information had been interpreted placed too much emphasis on direct military action and that a lot more could have been done to seek out terrorist groups before they struck.

Some politicians, both Democrats and Republicans, pointed out that the United States had been too complacent and that it had failed to realize that there were a lot of countries that simply did not trust the United States. It was in these countries that terrorists recruited new suicide bombers and worked toward the destruction of the United States and its friends and allies.

These politicians also pointed out that a fight against terrorism was also a fight against ignorance. They pointed out that reforms in intelligence gathering should take place alongside reforms in the way Americans did business in the world, building trust and cooperation.

After the Commission's findings were released, the government began to make changes to the ways the intelligence services are organized. The head of the CIA resigned, and several other senior officials changed positions or were moved to other agencies. More changes will take place over the next several years as the government adjusts the organization of these assets to counter any further attempts at terrorism.

One lesson has been learned, however. Never again can the United States believe that the two great oceans that brought its immigrants to populate the New World are a natural defense against its enemies.

President George W. Bush and Porter J. Goss hold a press conference at the Langley, Virginia, headquarters of the CIA on March 3, 2005.

Glossary

anarchist: a person who rebels against authority and the ruling power

anthrax: a serious disease of sheep and cattle that can be passed on to humans

assassination: the murder of an important person such as a president

Cold War: the standoff between the countries of the communist east and democratic west between 1945 and the early 1990s

counterfeiting: imitating something so that it looks exactly like the real thing

counterintelligence: activities designed to stop enemy spies

electronic: describes a device that contains transistors or silicon chips that control an electric current

espionage: the use of spies, often to gain military or political information

gangsterism: describes the activities of a group of organized criminals

Progressive: a political movement at the beginning of the 20th century that believed that the government should do more to help the individual and stop the corruption in some businesses

prohibition: the banning of something by law

remote: describes something that can be operated from some distance away

sabotage: to deliberately destroy, damage, or obstruct something to create difficulties for the enemy

satellite: device placed in orbit around the earth or any other planet and used to collect information

subversive: intending to destroy or completely ruin a government or organization

surveillance: the close observation of something

toxin: a poisonous substance

unconditionally: describes something that does not depend on anything else

Further Reading

Binns, Tristan. *The CIA (Government Agencies)*. Sagebrush, 2002

Binns, Tristan. *The FBI (Government Agencies)*. Sagebrush, 2002

Brennan, Kristine. *The Chernobyl Nuclear Disaster (Great Disasters)*. Chelsea House, 2002

Campbell, Geoffrey A. *A Vulnerable America (Lucent Library of Homeland Security)*. Lucent, 2003

Donovan, Sandra. *How Government Works: Protecting America*. Lerner Publishing Group, 2004

Gow, Mary. *Attack on America: The Day the Twin Towers Collapsed (American Disasters)*. Enslow Publishers, 2002

Hasan, Tahara. *Anthrax Attacks Around the World (Terrorist Attacks)*. Rosen Publishing Group, 2003

Katz, Samuel M. *Global Counterstrike: International Counterterrorism (Terrorist Dossiers)*. Lerner Publishing Group, 2004

Katz, Samuel M. *Targeting Terror: Counterterrorist Raids (Terrorist Dossiers)*. Lerner Publishing Group, 2004

Katz, Samuel M. *U.S. Counterstrike: American Counterterrorism (Terrorist Dossiers)*. Lerner Publishing Group, 2004

Margulies, Phillip. *Al-Qaeda: Osama Bin Laden's Army of Terrorists (Inside the World's Most Infamous Terrorist Organizations)*. Rosen Publishing Group, 2003

Marquette, Scott. *America Under Attack (America at War)*. Rourke Publishing LLC, 2003

Morris, Neil. *The Atlas of Islam*. Barron's, 2003

Owen, David. *Hidden Secrets: A Complete History of Espionage and the Technology Used to Support It.* Firefly Books Ltd, 2002

Ritchie, Jason. *Iraq and the Fall of Saddam Hussein.* Oliver Press, 2003

Websites to visit

The Central Intelligence Agency:
 www.cia.gov
The Department of Defense:
 www.defenselink.mil
The Department of Homeland Security:
 www.dhs.gov
The Federal Bureau of Investigation:
 www.fbi.gov
The U.S. Air Force:
 www.af.mil
The U.S. Army
 www.army.mil

The U.S. Coast Guard:
 www.uscg.mil
The U.S. Government Official Website:
 www.firstgov.gov
The U.S. Marine Corps:
 www.usmc.mil
The U.S. Navy:
 www.navy.mil
The U.S. Secret Service:
 www.secretservice.gov
The White House:
 www.whitehouse.gov

Index